Fun & Fabulous

Grain-Free

Breakfast Recipes

How to Enjoy Your Old Favorites in a

Brand New Way!

- *Eggs & Toast!*

- *Pancakes & Waffles!*

- *Muffins & More!*

By Lisa Bishop

www.grainfreerecipes.com

Find more information on grain-free living at

www.grainfreerecipes.com

Your Health is Your Responsibility – IMPORTANT DISCLAIMER

Published by
Full Timer Press, LLC
www.grainfreerecipes.com
fulltimerpress@gmail.com

Table of Contents

Why This Book Was Written...4

My Story 5

The Grain Free Pantry...6

Milk Free – Egg Free..7

Eggs, Anyone? 8

Mmm, Casseroles! 15

Heavenly Hash Browns 21

Finally, Pancakes! 26

Biscuit, Bread and Muffins, Oh My!.....................................32

Cereal and Milk!...40

Other Good Stuff! 46

Why This Book Was Written

It has been my pleasure to work for almost 20 years with my father, James T. Bishop, MD, a Stanford-trained physician who specializes in Food and Respiratory Allergy. During that time, helping food allergic patients, including my children and myself, it became very apparent to the both of us that the main difficulty most folks have with staying on a grain-free diet is breakfast.

Dinner and lunch are easy – a salad, veggie and grilled chicken, fish or steak will do it. But breakfast on an ongoing basis proves much more challenging. What do you eat when you get tired of scrambled eggs? How do you satisfy your craving for toast with your coffee in the morning? What about waffles, pancakes and cereal?

This book is a solution to your problem. All the recipes listed here are grain, gluten and potato free. Additionally, minimal sweeteners are used. Although many recipes were tested for this book, only those that passed certain stringent requirements can be found here. For one thing, each recipe had to pass the rigorous taste tests of our local experts: 13 year-old Jacob, 11 year-old Madeline, 2 ½ year-old Ellie, and my husband Phil (who absolutely loves baked goods).

In addition, the recipes had to be easy to fix. Most of the recipes were originally tested in the kitchen of our fifth wheel camper while my husband and I were out on the road, exploring this great country with our kids. This kitchen had only one foot of counter space and a teeny-tiny stove and oven, so these recipes can be made pretty much anywhere. I hope you like them as much as we do.

My Story

I am allergic to quite a few foods, including wheat, corn, and potato. I experience moderate to severe symptoms when I eat these foods, from severe headaches, achy joints, and puffy fingers to falling into a food coma after I eat and waking up in the middle of the night with reflux so bad I can barely breathe. I don't feel well and tend to be crabby with my family.

Even with these repercussions, I still find it exceedingly difficult to stay off of these foods, due to their highly addictive nature and their prominent use in most processed goods. One thing to know about food allergies is, if you crave a food and have to have it – can't imagine life without eating it - that's a pretty strong signal that you are allergic, or at least have a very high sensitivity, to it.

Eating a grain-free diet makes a huge improvement in my life on a daily basis. When I am off grain, I feel so much better. My symptoms all disappear fairly quickly. The chronic headaches are gone, and I have much more energy. My rings start to loosen, and even my face feels thinner after a few days, which is a very good thing.

My family members have food allergies as well, with symptoms ranging from dark under eye circles, excess saliva, nasal stuffiness, foggy thinking and general crankiness to gas pains in my toddler that are bad enough to keep us up all night. Even my husband feels sick when he eats eggs. Finding foods we can all tolerate can be a challenge.

Having these recipes available, which are easy to make and good to eat, makes it easy for our family to start the day symptom-free. It is my sincere wish that these recipes make as big a difference in your life as they have in mine.

The Grain Free Pantry

Some of the recipes may contain ingredients you are unfamiliar with. or have not used before. Have no fear, they are all easy to work with and are pretty easy to find. Most of these items can be found in any high-end grocery store, or well stocked health food store. Many can also be ordered (sometimes cheaper) through **GrainFreeRecipes.com**.

Agave Nectar: Agave is a natural nectar made from of the Agave plant. Agave Nectar has a Low Glycemic Index, so it is slowly absorbed into the body, preventing spikes in blood sugar. Find it next to the honey at your local health food store.

Almond butter: This nut butter can be made yourself by grinding almonds in a blender to a butter consistency. I buy mine already made. Some grocery stores do carry it; otherwise, get it at your health food store.

Almond flour: Almond flour is made from grinding raw almonds. You can grind it yourself in a blender, or purchase it already ground. It is full of protein and dietary fiber, and works well in a wide array of recipes.

Amaranth flour: This flour is made from grinding amaranth seeds. Amaranth is sometimes called a pseudo-grain because of its flavor and cooking similarity to grains.

Chickpea flour: Chickpea flour is made from chickpeas (also known as garbanzo beans) and is high in protein.

Coconut, shredded, unsweetened: Most grocery stores carry the sweetened version, which you do not want to use. Look for the unsweetened version in your local health food store.

Coconut flour: Coconut flour is high in fiber and a good source of protein.

Flaxseed meal: Made from ground flax seeds, this meal should be used fairly quickly, to prevent rancidity. I found mine at Wal-Mart next to the flours in the baking section.

Jicama: (Pronounced hick-a-ma) A root vegetable known for its very crunchy, apple-like and mild flavor. Find it in the refrigerated produce section at your grocery store.

Milk Free – Egg Free

	Milk Free	Egg Free	Page Number
Banana Eggs	X		14
Hash Browns	X	X	22
Crunchy Hash Browns	X		23
Zucchini Hash	X		24
Fake Fried Potatoes	X	X	25
Almond Pancakes	X		27
Very Berry Pancakes	X		29
Fabulous Flax Bread	X		34
Oh So Quick Bread	X		35
Shorty Bread		X	36
Fry It In A Skillet Bread	X	X	37
Hot Apple Cereal	X	X	41
Kitchen Sink Cereal	X		42
Amazing Amaranth	X	X	43
Groovy Granola	X	X	44
Nutty Milk	X	X	45
Jeannie's Breakfast		X	47
Granola Bars		X	48
Drink Your Greens Smoothie	X	X	49
Peppered Strawberries	X	X	51
Acorn Squash	X	X	52
Almond Madness	X	X	53
Banana Wrap	X	X	54

Eggs, Anyone?

EZ Egg Cakes 9

Two Minute Eggs 10

Dr. B's Favorite Omelette 11

Bird Nests 12

Easy Cheezy..13

Banana Eggs..14

EZ Egg Cakes

These poof up like little soufflés, then fall as they cool.
Easy and fast.
The kids loved them.
These freeze well. Just pop in the microwave for a minute and voila!
Add cooked sausage, bacon or veggies into the eggs for variety.

Ingredients:

- 6 eggs
- ½ cup cream
- 6 oz shredded cheese
- Salt and pepper to taste

Directions:

1. Spray a muffin tin with non-stick spray.
2. Beat the eggs, cream, salt and pepper in a bowl with a fork.
3. Pour into the muffin tins, filling the tins only halfway.
4. Add ½ oz of shredded cheese on each top.
5. Bake at 350°F for 15 minutes or until golden brown.

Shopping:

Dairy: eggs
cream
shredded cheese

Pantry: salt
pepper

Two Minute Eggs

These are really quick and easy!
Makes a single serving.

Ingredients:

- 2 eggs
- 1 slice American cheese
- Salt and pepper to taste

Directions:

1. Beat the eggs with a fork in a microwave safe bowl.
2. Microwave for 1 minute.
3. Stir eggs and top with cheese.
4. Microwave for another minute or until done.
5. Season with salt and pepper to taste.

Shopping:

Dairy: eggs
        American cheese

Pantry: salt
        pepper

Dr. B's Favorite Omelette

No breakfast recipe book should be without at least one omelette recipe!
Dr. B would eat this everyday if he could!

Ingredients:

- Eggbeaters
- Bacon Bits
- goat cheese
- ½ avocado
- Sliced tomatoes

Directions:

1. Cook Eggbeaters omelette style.
2. Fill with Bacon Bits, goat cheese and avocado.
3. Flip and serve with sliced tomatoes on top.

Shopping:

Dairy:	Eggbeaters
	goat cheese
Meat:	Bacon Bits
Produce:	tomatoes
	avocado

Bird Nests

These are good!
They also work well with Egg Beaters.

Ingredients:

- 6 eggs
- 6 pieces thinly sliced ham
- 1 tablespoon half & half or heavy cream
- ½ cup shredded cheddar cheese
- ¼ cup diced onion
- ½ teaspoon salt
- ½ teaspoon pepper

Directions:

1. Spray a muffin tin with non-stick spray.
2. Place a ham slice in each muffin tin.
3. In a medium bowl, beat together the remaining ingredients.
4. Fill each tin with ½ cup of the egg mixture.
5. Bake at 375°F for 20-25 minutes.

Options:

For a simplified version, crack an egg into each ham cup and top with shredded cheese. Bake as specified. This tastes like a hard-boiled egg!

Shopping:

Dairy:	eggs
	cream
	cheddar cheese
Meat:	ham
Pantry:	salt
	pepper
Produce:	onion

Easy Cheezy

Quick and easy!

Ingredients:

- 1 cup chopped, cooked ham
- 4 eggs
- ¼ cup chopped red pepper
- ⅓ cup chopped onion
- ½ cup shredded cheddar cheese
- 1 tablespoon butter
- Salt and pepper to taste

Directions:

1. Microwave the butter in a glass pie plate until melted.
2. Lay the ham, red pepper and onion evenly in the pie plate.
3. Microwave for two minutes.
4. In a separate bowl, beat the eggs with salt and pepper.
5. Pour into meat mixture and stir evenly.
6. Microwave 3-6 minutes, or until eggs are cooked.
7. Top with the cheese.
8. Microwave 30 seconds or until the cheese melts.
9. Let stand a few minutes before serving.

Shopping:

Dairy:	eggs
	cheddar cheese
	butter
Pantry:	salt
	pepper
Meat:	ham
Produce:	green pepper
	onion

Banana Eggs

The kids like these with a bit of sugar-free maple syrup on top!

Ingredients:

- 3 eggs
- 1 banana
- 1 tablespoon Agave or Splenda
- 1 teaspoon butter or coconut oil
- 1 teaspoon cinnamon
- 1 pinch salt

Directions:

1. Add the eggs, banana, Agave, cinnamon and salt in a blender.
2. Blend until smooth.
3. Melt butter or coconut oil in a non-stick pan over medium heat. (Do not skip this!)
4. Add the egg mixture and cook until the eggs begin to set.
5. Flip and cook until the eggs are done.

Shopping:

Dairy:	eggs
	butter or coconut oil
Pantry:	Agave or Splenda
	cinnamon
	salt
Produce:	banana

Mmm, Casseroles!

Creamy Custard..*16*

Comforting Quiche *17*

Baked Omelette Squares *18*

So Sausage Scramble...*19*

Lotsa Meat Pie..*20*

Creamy Custard

Fabulous!
This is so smooth and well worth the time to make.
Add flavorings, nuts and berries for different combinations.
Serves one.

Ingredients:

- 2 eggs
- ½ cup cream
- 2 tablespoon Agave
- Splash of vanilla

Directions:

1. Preheat the oven to 300°F
2. Whisk the ingredients in a small, ovenproof bowl.
3. Place the bowl in a large pan filled with water.
4. Bake for 60 minutes.

Shopping:

Dairy: eggs
                cream

Pantry: Agave Nectar
                vanilla

Comforting Quiche

So easy!
Pop leftovers in the microwave for a minute for a quick meal.
Add ¾ cup of cooked meat or veggies for variety.
Buy disposable pie plates and make up several different kinds of quiches at once.
Bake, slice and freeze. Then you have a variety to eat during the week.

Ingredients:

- 6 eggs
- 1 pint heavy cream
- 2 cups shredded cheese
- Salt and pepper to taste

Directions:

1. Preheat the oven to 350°F.
2. Beat together all the ingredients in a bowl.
3. Pour into a pie pan.
4. Bake 40 minutes or until a toothpick comes out clean.

Shopping:

Dairy:	eggs
	cream
	cheese
Pantry:	salt
	pepper

Baked Omelette Squares

Good and easy!

Ingredients:

- 10 eggs
- ¼ cup heavy cream
- 4 oz shredded cheddar cheese
- ½ cup diced bell pepper
- 2 tablespoons minced onion
- 4 oz cooked, diced ham
- ¼ teaspoon salt

Directions:

1. Preheat the oven to 350˚F.
2. In a medium bowl, beat together the eggs and cream.
3. Add all other ingredients and mix well.
4. Pour the mixture into an 8 x 8 glass pan.
5. Bake for 40 minutes.
6. Cut into pieces and serve hot.

Shopping:

Dairy:	eggs
	cream
	cheddar cheese
Meat:	ham
Pantry:	salt
Produce:	bell pepper
	onion

So Sausage Scramble

So creamy and comforting!

Ingredients:

- 1 lb bulk sausage, mild or spicy
- 6 eggs
- 6 oz cream cheese
- ½ cup diced onion
- 2 tablespoons water

Directions:

1. Brown the sausage and onions together.
2. Add cream cheese and cook on low until melted.
3. Wisk the eggs and water together.
4. Add to sausage mixture.
5. Cook until done, stirring constantly.

Shopping:

Dairy:	eggs
	cream cheese
Meat:	bulk sausage
Produce:	onion

Lotsa Meat Pie

Hubby considers this great comfort food.

Ingredients:

- 5 eggs
- 1 lb bulk Italian sausage
- 8 oz mozzarella cheese
- ½ cup diced red bell pepper
- ½ cup diced yellow onion
- ½ cup diced zucchini or yellow squash
- 1 teaspoon garlic powder
- 1 teaspoon oregano
- Dash cayenne pepper
- Salt and pepper to taste

Directions:

1. Preheat the oven to 350°F.
2. Brown the sausage and onion.
3. Drain the fat.
4. Beat the eggs in a large bowl.
5. Add the sausage and onion and all other ingredients and mix well.
6. Spray a 9" pie plate with non-stick spray
7. Spread egg mixture onto pie plate.
8. Bake for 30 minutes, or until lightly browned on top.

Shopping:

Dairy:	eggs mozzarella cheese		
Meat:	Italian sausage		
Pantry:	garlic powder salt	oregano pepper	cayenne pepper
Produce:	red bell pepper yellow onion	zucchini or yellow squash	

Heavenly Hash Browns

Hash Browns 22

Crunchy Hash Browns 23

Zucchini Hash...24

Fake Fried Potatoes...25

Hash Browns

These are a nice alternative to potatoes.

Ingredients:

- ½ head chopped cauliflower (fresh, not frozen)
- ½ cup chopped green pepper
- ½ cup chopped onion
- 1 ½ tablespoons cooking oil*
- ½ teaspoon Lawry's Seasoning Salt

Directions:

1. Melt the butter in a skillet.
2. Make sure the veggies are dry, and then add to the skillet with seasoning.
3. Stir well to coat all the veggies.
4. Cook on medium/high heat stirring often.
5. Cook for 6-10 minutes or until browned.
6. Best served hot.

*Note: For added flavor, substitute 1 tablespoon of butter and 1 teaspoon cooking oil.

Shopping:

Pantry: cooking oil
Lawry's seasoning salt

Produce: cauliflower
green pepper
onion

Crunchy Hash Browns

Jacob said these smell just like McDonald's.
All the kids loved them!
These are quick and easy to fix.

Ingredients:

- 2 cups coleslaw mix (find pre-bagged next to the bag lettuce in your grocery store)
- 1 chopped green onion
- 1 egg
- 1 tablespoon canola oil
- Salt and pepper to taste

Directions:

1. Combine the Cole slaw mix, green onion, egg, salt and pepper.
2. Mix thoroughly.
3. Heat the canola oil in a skillet over medium-high heat.
4. Form the coleslaw mix into loose patties and fry.
5. When browned, flip and brown the other side.
6. Serve hot.

Shopping:

Dairy: egg

Pantry: canola oil
               salt
               pepper

Produce: coleslaw mix
               green onion

Zucchini Hash

These are a little on the sweet side.
They could pass for pancakes as well.

Ingredients:

- 1 cup grated zucchini
- 2 beaten eggs
- 1 tablespoon grated onion
- 1 tablespoon canola oil
- Dash of garlic powder
- Dash of onion powder
- Salt and pepper to taste

Directions:

1. Add all of the ingredients except for the canola oil in a bowl.
2. Mix thoroughly.
3. Heat the canola oil in a skillet over medium-high heat.
4. Form the zucchini mixture into loose patties and fry.
5. When browned, flip and brown the other side.
6. Serve hot.

Shopping:

Dairy: eggs

Pantry: canola oil
                onion powder
                garlic powder
                salt
                pepper

Produce: zucchini
                onion

Fake Fried Potatoes

These crunchy tidbits are great with eggs in the morning!

Ingredients:

- 1 cup peeled, diced jicama
- ¼ cup diced onion
- 1 tablespoon canola oil
- 1 teaspoon poultry seasoning
- Salt and pepper to taste

Directions:

1. Heat canola oil in a skillet over medium-high heat.
2. Add the jicama, onion and poultry seasoning to skillet.
3. Mix well.
4. Brown the mixture, stirring occasionally.
5. Add salt and pepper to taste.
6. Serve hot.

Shopping:

Pantry: canola oil
                 poultry seasoning
                 salt
                 pepper

Produce: jicama
                 onion

Finally, Pancakes!

Almond Pancakes..*27*

I Want More! Pancakes *28*

Very Berry Pancakes *29*

Oh My Word! Waffles *30*

French Toast Omelette...*31*

Almond Pancakes

Awesome!
These look and taste like multi-grain pancakes.

Ingredients:

- 2 eggs
- 1 cup almond flour
- ¼ cup water
- 1 tablespoon Agave nectar or Splenda
- 2 tablespoons oil
- Sugar-free maple syrup

Directions:

1. Mix all of the ingredients except the maple syrup together.
2. Preheat a non-stick pan over medium-low heat.
3. Pour in a small pancake and flip when the underside is golden brown.
4. Serve with sugar-free maple syrup.

Shopping:

Dairy: eggs

Pantry: almond flour
             Agave Nectar or Splenda
             oil
             sugar-free maple syrup

I Want More! Pancakes

Yummy!
All the kids gave this recipe double thumbs-up!

Ingredients:

- 2 eggs
- 1 teaspoon butter
- 4 oz cream cheese
- 1 tablespoon flax seed meal (optional)
- ½ teaspoon cinnamon
- 3 single serving packets Splenda
- 1 dash salt
- sugar-free maple syrup

Directions:

1. Beat egg whites until stiff peaks appear, then set aside.
2. Beat together the remaining ingredients until smooth.
3. Fold in the egg whites.
4. Preheat a non-stick pan over medium-low heat.
5. Pour a small pancake and flip when the underside is golden brown.
6. Serve with sugar-free maple syrup.

Shopping:

Dairy: eggs
        butter
        cream cheese

Pantry: flax seed meal (optional)
        Splenda
        sugar-free maple syrup
        cinnamon
        salt

Very Berry Pancakes

Madeline had seconds.
Ellie ate them plain.
Need I say more?

Ingredients:

- 2 eggs
- 2 tablespoons sifted coconut flour
- ½ cup fresh blueberries
- 2 tablespoons melted butter (or coconut oil)
- 2 tablespoons milk (or nut, coconut or soy milk)
- 1 teaspoon Splenda
- 1/8 teaspoon salt
- 1/8 teaspoon baking powder
- sugar-free maple syrup

Directions:

1. Combine all ingredients except the blueberries and mix well.
2. Gently fold in the blueberries.
3. Preheat a non-stick pan over medium-low heat.
4. Pour a small pancake size and turn when underside is golden brown.
5. Serve with lots of sugar-free maple syrup.

Shopping:

Dairy:	eggs
	milk (or, nut, coconut or soy)
	butter (or coconut oil)
Pantry:	coconut flour
	baking powder
	Splenda
	salt
	sugar-free syrup
Produce:	blueberries

Oh My Word! Waffles

Oh my word, are these good!
They taste like doughnuts.
You can also cook these as pancakes or muffins.

Ingredients:

- 1 cup almond flour
- 1 cup flax seed meal
- 1 cup Splenda
- 4 eggs
- ½ cup butter
- ½ cup plus 2 tablespoons water
- 1 teaspoon cinnamon
- ¼ teaspoon salt
- ¼ teaspoon allspice (optional)

Directions:

1. Melt the butter in a large bowl.
2. Add eggs and water, stir.
3. Add all other ingredients and mix well.
4. Cook in waffle iron until done.

Shopping:

Dairy: eggs
                butter

Pantry: almond flour
                flax seed meal
                Splenda
                cinnamon
                allspice (optional)
                salt

French Toast Omelette

Very good!
Great for a sweet tooth!

Ingredients:

- 4 eggs
- ¼ cup heavy cream
- 2 tablespoons Splenda
- 1 teaspoon maple extract
- 2 teaspoons cinnamon
- sugar-free syrup

Directions:

1. Combine all the ingredients in a bowl.
2. Cook like an omelette.
3. Top with sugar-free syrup.

Shopping:

Dairy: eggs
                cream

Pantry: Splenda
                maple extract
                cinnamon
                sugar-free syrup

Biscuit, Bread and Muffins, Oh My!

Simply Biscuits *33*

Fabulous Flax Bread *34*

Oh So Quick Bread *35*

Shorty Bread *36*

Fry It In a Skillet Bread *37*

Apple a Day Muffins *38*

Cheesy Muffins *39*

Simply Biscuits

Madeline thinks these taste like French fries.
They are awesome topped with sugar-free raspberry jam.

Ingredients:

- 1 egg
- 2 cups almond flour
- ½ teaspoon salt
- ½ cup softened butter

Directions:

1. Preheat the oven to 325°F.
2. Line a baking sheet with parchment paper.
3. Combine almond flour, salt, egg and salt.
4. Mix with your hands because the dough will be stiff.
5. Make 2-tablespoon sized balls of dough and flatten them slightly with your hands.
6. Bake for 18 to 20 minutes.

Shopping:

Dairy:	eggs
	butter
Pantry:	almond flour
	salt

Fabulous Flax Bread

Great for sandwiches or toasting.

Ingredients:

- 2 cups flax seed meal
- 5 eggs
- ¾ cup water
- 2 tablespoons Splenda
- ¼ teaspoon baking powder
- ¼ teaspoon salt

Directions:

1. Preheat the oven to 350°F.
2. Spray pan* with nonstick spray.
3. Beat eggs and water together.
4. Add all other ingredients and mix well.
5. Let batter sit for two minutes.
6. Pour batter into the pan.
7. Bake for 20-25 minutes, or until the top springs back when you touch it.

* Note: A 10x15 pan with sides will give you Focaccia style, or you can use a loaf pan.

Shopping:

Dairy:	eggs
Pantry:	flax seed meal
	Splenda
	baking powder
	salt

Oh So Quick Bread

This is so easy and quick.
Good for toast and sandwiches.

Ingredients:

- 1 cup almond flour
- ¾ cup water
- 2 eggs
- ¼ teaspoon salt
- ½ teaspoon baking soda

Directions:

1. Combine all ingredients and mix well.
2. Pour into a microwavable dish with straight sides.
3. Microwave for about 5 minutes, or until the top springs back when touched.
4. Turn upside down on a flat surface to cool.
5. If desired, put upside down back into pan and microwave for another two minutes to make the bottom surface drier.

Note: For denser bread, use up to 2 ½ cups of almond flour and cook a bit longer.

Shopping:

Dairy: eggs

Pantry: almond flour
                baking soda
                salt

Shorty Bread

This is yummy and so easy!
It is great plain or topped with sugar-free jam.

Ingredients:

- 6 tablespoons melted butter
- 2 cups almond flour
- 2 ½ tablespoons Agave Nectar
- Canola oil

Directions:

1. Preheat the oven to 350˚F.
2. Combine all the ingredients in a bowl.
3. Press the dough into a 9" pie or cake tin.
4. Prick the top with a fork.
5. Bake for 15 to 20 minutes or until golden brown.
6. Let cool in the pan and then cut into wedges.

Shopping:

Dairy: butter

Pantry: almond flour
                Agave Nectar
                canola oil

Fry It in a Skillet Bread

Easy!
This is very good with sugar-free jam.

Ingredients:

- ½ cup chick-pea (garbanzo bean) flour
- ⅔ cup water
- 1 teaspoon salt

Directions:

1. Mix all ingredients in a bowl.
2. It should be a very thin batter. If not, add a little more water.
3. Heat a 12" non-stick pan over medium-high heat until a drop of water will dance on the surface.
4. Add 1 teaspoon oil and coat bottom.
5. Pour all the batter into the pan and cover.
6. Cook for 5 minutes or until the edges look dry.
7. Flip and reduce heat to medium-low.
8. Cook uncovered 5 minutes.
9. Serve immediately.

Shopping:

Pantry: chickpea flour
               salt

Apple a Day Muffins

Grandma thought these were great!

Ingredients:

- 2 eggs
- ½ cup melted butter
- 1 cup almond flour
- 1 large, peeled and diced apple
- ¼ cup unsweetened applesauce
- ¼ cup Agave Nectar
- ¼ teaspoon baking soda
- 1 teaspoon vanilla
- cinnamon to taste

Directions:

1. Preheat the oven to 325°F.
2. Combine all ingredients except cinnamon in a bowl.
3. Pour batter into lined muffin tins and sprinkle cinnamon on top.
4. Bake for 20-25 minutes, or until the tops are golden brown.

Shopping:

Dairy:	eggs
	butter
Pantry:	almond flour
	applesauce
	Agave Nectar
	baking soda
	vanilla
	cinnamon
Produce:	apple

Cheesy Muffins

The toddler ate two of these!

Ingredients:

- 1 cup almond flour
- 1 cup cream
- 2 eggs
- 1 tablespoon melted butter
- ½ cup shredded cheddar cheese
- ¼ teaspoon salt

Directions:

1. Preheat the oven to 425˚F.
2. Spray 8 muffin cups with nonstick spray.
3. Combine flour, cream, eggs, butter and salt together until smooth.
4. Fold in the cheddar cheese.
5. Pour into muffin cups.
6. Bake for 15 minutes.
7. Reduce heat to 350˚F and bake an additional 25 minutes or until tops are golden brown.

Shopping:

Dairy: eggs
                cream
                butter
                cheddar cheese

Pantry: almond flour
                salt

Cereal and Milk!

Hot Apple Cereal 41

Kitchen Sink Cereal 42

Amazing Amaranth 43

Groovy Granola...44

Nutty Milk...45

Hot Apple Cereal

Warm and so yummy!
This is also good cold.

Ingredients:

- 2 chopped apples
- ¼ cup chopped nuts
- 2 handfuls raisins
- 2 pinches sea salt
- cinnamon to taste
- Agave Nectar to taste

Directions:

1. Combine all the ingredients in a pot.
2. Cook on medium heat until apples are soft.
3. Stir occasionally.

Shopping:

Pantry: nuts
             raisins
             cinnamon
             Agave Nectar
             salt

Produce: apples

Kitchen Sink Cereal

Quick, good, and never boring!

Ingredients:

- 1 egg
- ¼ cup flax seed meal
- ¼ cup water (or sugar-free syrup)
- Splenda to taste
- additions*

Directions:

1. Beat egg in small dish.
2. Mix in water and flax seed meal.
3. Microwave for 45 seconds.
4. Stir and add in any additional ingredients.
5. Microwave for another minute, until done.

*Note: The variations to this cereal are unlimited. Try adding in any of the following: dried, fresh or frozen fruit, sugar-free syrups, nuts, sugar-free jam, coconut, cinnamon or vanilla and other extracts.

Shopping:

Dairy: egg

Pantry: flax seed meal
                Splenda
                additions*

Amazing Amaranth

This is a great substitute for oatmeal.
It has a consistency that is a bit like Malt-O-Meal.
Make it at night and reheat in the morning!

Ingredients:

- 1 cup amaranth
- 3 cups water
- 2 tablespoons Agave Nectar
- Sprinkle of cinnamon
- Splash of coconut or almond milk (optional)

Directions:

1. Mix the amaranth and water in a pot.
2. Heat to boiling.
3. Reduce heat and simmer for 25 minutes, stirring occasionally.
4. Mix in the Agave Nectar.
5. Sprinkle with cinnamon.
6. Splash coconut milk on top.

Shopping:

Pantry: amaranth
coconut or almond milk (optional)
Agave Nectar
cinnamon

Groovy Granola

This is great with almond milk poured over it, or just grab a handful and go!

Ingredients:

- 1 ½ cup amaranth flour
- 1 cup husked sunflower seeds
- 1 cup chopped walnuts or other nuts
- 1 cup grated unsweetened coconut
- 1 mashed banana
- 2/3 cup raisins
- 1/3 cup canola or walnut oil
- ¼ cup Agave Nectar
- 1 tablespoon lemon juice
- 1 ½ teaspoons vanilla extract
- 1 ½ teaspoons cinnamon

Directions:

1. Preheat the oven to 300°F.
2. Mix the banana, oil, Agave Nectar, lemon juice and vanilla in a small bowl. Set aside.
3. Mix all other ingredients in a large bowl.
4. Add the liquid ingredients to the dry ones and mix thoroughly.
5. Spray a large pan or cookie sheet with non-stick spray.
6. Spread mixture into pan.
7. Bake 60 minutes, stirring every 15 minutes.

Shopping:

Pantry:	amaranth flour	sunflower seeds
	walnuts	unsweetened coconut
	raisins	canola oil
	Agave Nectar	vanilla extract
	cinnamon	
Produce:	banana	
	lemon juice	

Nutty Milk

This is a nice alternative to cow's milk.
Use on grain-free granola, in your coffee or tea, or just straight.
You can get quite a variety by trying different nuts and seeds.

Ingredients:

- 3 cups of water (use less water for richer, creamier milk)
- 1 cup raw almonds (or other nuts or seeds)
- 1 tablespoon Agave Nectar or 2-3 dates
- 1 teaspoon salt

Directions:

1. Place all of the ingredients in a blender and blend until smooth.
2. Strain through a cheesecloth or nut bag, retaining liquid.
3. Chill and drink.

Shopping:

Pantry: almonds
                Agave nectar or dates
                salt

Other Good Stuff!

Jeannie's Breakfast 47

Granola Bars 48

Drink Your Greens Smoothie 49

Breakfast Balls 50

Peppered Strawberries 51

Acorn Squash 52

Almond Madness 53

Banana Wrap 54

Jeannie's Breakfast

My friend Jeanne would make this once a week and cut a piece each morning for a quick, sweet start to her day.

Ingredients:

- 1 pkg sugar-free Jell-O
- 1 container low carb yogurt
- 1 cup fruit
- hot water

Directions:

1. Combine the Jell-O with hot water as directed on the package.
2. Add yogurt, fruit and mix well.
3. Chill until firm.

Shopping:

Dairy:	low carb yogurt
Pantry:	sugar-free Jell-O
Produce:	fruit

Granola Bars

These are good and sweet.

Ingredients:

- 1 ¼ cup pecans
- 1 cup unsweetened, shredded coconut
- ½ cup raisins
- 2 tablespoons Agave Nectar
- ½ tablespoon soft butter
- 1 teaspoon vanilla
- 1/8 teaspoon salt

Directions:

1. Preheat the oven to 300°F.
2. Blend all of the ingredients together in a food processor until smooth, but leave a little texture.
3. Spray a 9x9 pan with non-stick spray.
4. Press evenly into the pan.
5. Bake 15 minutes or until lightly browned.
6. Let cool and cut into squares.

Shopping:

Dairy:	butter
Pantry:	coconut
	pecans
	raisins
	Agave nectar
	vanilla
	salt

Drink Your Greens Smoothie

This is a fabulous way to add dark, leafy greens to your diet.
It is definitely kid-approved! (You can't taste the spinach – trust me!)
Add fresh or frozen blueberries to make a nice mud color for the kids!

Ingredients:

- 1 large handful of fresh, raw spinach (or more as you get braver)
- 1 banana
- 3 cups water
- 2-4 cups frozen mixed fruit, no sugar added

Directions:

1. In your blender, combine spinach, banana and 2 cups of water. Blend.
2. Add enough frozen fruit so the blender is ¾ full.
3. Add 1 cup of water.
4. Blend on low and gradually increase speed until thoroughly blended.
5. Add more or less water to make the consistency of your smoothie thicker or thinner.
6. Enjoy immediately, preferably with a bright colorful straw.

Shopping:

Frozen: mixed fruit

Produce: spinach
               banana

Breakfast Balls

The whole family asked for seconds and thirds.
They freeze well.
Pull out a few in the morning and pop in the microwave for a quick and hearty breakfast.

Ingredients:

- 2 lbs bulk breakfast sausage
- 1 lb ground turkey
- 3 eggs
- 2 cups shredded, sharp cheddar cheese
- 1/3 cup minced onion
- Pepper to taste

Directions:

1. Preheat the oven to 350°F.
2. Mix all ingredients together in a large bowl.
3. Drop by spoonfuls onto a cookie sheet or roll into 1½" balls.
4. Bake 20 minutes.
5. Serve with low sugar barbeque sauce.

Shopping:

Dairy:	eggs
	cheddar cheese
Meat:	bulk sausage
	ground turkey
Pantry:	pepper
Produce:	onion

Peppered Strawberries

Fabulous.
The kids liked this once I convinced them to try it!

Ingredients:

- 1 lb washed, hulled and sliced strawberries
- 4 teaspoons balsamic vinegar
- cracked black pepper, to taste

Directions:

1. Place the strawberries into a medium bowl.
2. Add the balsamic vinegar and cracked black pepper.
3. Toss well and serve.

Shopping:

Produce: strawberries

Pantry: balsamic vinegar
cracked black pepper

Acorn Squash

This is simple, quick and so good.
It will make your kitchen smell fabulous.
It is also great cold!

Ingredients:

- 1 acorn squash
- 2 tablespoons raisins
- 2 tablespoons chopped nuts
- sugar-free maple syrup

Directions:

1. Place squash on microwave safe plate.
2. Microwave four minutes.
3. Turn over and microwave another four minutes, or until easily pierced with a fork.
4. Cut in half and scrape out the seeds.
5. Top with raisins and chopped nuts.
6. Drizzle with sugar-free maple syrup.

Shopping:

Pantry: sugar-free maple syrup
squash
raisins
nuts

Almond Madness

Madeline loves this for breakfast, dessert, anytime!
A great comfort food.
If you can tolerate the sugar, try it with real maple syrup!

Ingredients:

- 1 sliced banana
- ½ cup almond butter
- ½ cup unsweetened, shredded coconut
- ½ cup sugar-free maple syrup or Agave Nectar

Directions:

1. Combine banana, almond butter and coconut in a bowl.
2. Drizzle with sugar-free maple syrup or Agave Nectar.

Shopping:

Pantry: almond butter
shredded coconut
sugar-free maple syrup or Agave Nectar

Produce: banana

Banana Wrap

This is crunchy, sweet and quick!
Dot almond butter on the inside of the leaf before wrapping to give it a different twist.

Ingredients:

- 1 ripe banana
- 1 large leaf of romaine lettuce

Directions:

1. Wrap the banana in the romaine leaf.
2. Eat and enjoy!

Shopping:

Produce: banana
              romaine lettuce

13322831R00031

Made in the USA
Lexington, KY
25 January 2012